"*Terrible Grace* is a stunning and surreal carnival, where "the next tent/ is ten shades of blackstrap dim" and the family is made up of the "exquisitely broken and extraterrestrial interlopers". I admire this poetry's astounding images and well-made lines and the way the two voices blend and diverge. I'm taken by their close attentions to the mysteries of fatherhood and gender, the mystery of love, not to mention language itself: "...cold enough to see our breath we made language in the tall grass on the days the words won't come we hold hands."

-Joseph Millar, Author of *Kingdom: Carnegie-Mellon Poetry Series* and *Dark Harvest:* Eastern Washington University Press.

"Who, reading these poems, won't catch a glimpse of themselves in the mocked and misunderstood lives disclosed here? The two poets' conjoined visions allow us not only to meet a carnival of "exquisitely broken" beings, but to slip inside their skins and share what burns in their interiors, from disdain for ignorant gawkers to the fierce will to be alive. And we may need to ask if there's something in us, too, of the crowds of clueless onlookers estranged from their own souls. Otherness blazes in this collection. Alligator Woman "lights a fire with her tail." A father assures his son that "God has many plans and we/are two of them." The two halves of the book, like conjoined twins Wilbur and Stanley, feed each other. Mystery and awe coupled with lush, unexpected language lights fires in the imagination."

-Joan Larkin, author of *My Body: New and Selected Poems:* Hanging Loose Press

"In Paul Koneicki and Christopher Soden's *Terrible Grace* we find a collaboration of empathy, intelligence, and beauty. These poems which move in the American tradition of Persona go beyond simply dreaming into another's life. A dream that in less skilled hands would stop at the surprise of seeing someone or something that was different than themselves. Instead Koneicki and Soden join the likes of poets like AI who are not only inspired by their subjects but write through a voice that humanizes and illuminates them. At turns lyrical and masterfully narrative, this collection is a bit of grace focused on an often terrible moment of our history."

-Matthew Dickman, Author of *Wonderland,* W. W. Norton and Company

"I've heard rumblings about this project for a long time now & it doesn't disappoint. Koniecki & Soden's *Terrible Grace* is the perfect literary pairing of contemporary American poets, both surreal & starkly realistic, like the writers themselves, the book puts some distance between two lives held so close together, yet at times so far apart, while allowing them to remain whole."

-John Dorsey, Author of *Sundown at the Redneck Carnival,* Spartan Press

Terrible Grace

Poems by Paul Koniecki and
Christopher Stephen Soden

LUCHADOR
PRESS

Luchador Press
Big Tuna, TX

Copyright © 2022, Paul Koniecki, Christopher Stephen Soden

First Edition: 1 3 5 7 9 10 8 6 4 2

ISBN: 978-1-958182-03-1

LCCN: 2022938674

Author photos: Paul Koniecki, Christopher Stephen Soden

Acknowledgments:

Wilbur and Stanley appeared in Issue #5 of *Impossible Archetypes*, an online LGBTQ Journal March 25th, 2019. Editor Mark Ward.

— — — — —

The first half of the book is written in the voice of Adam Rainer's mother. Adam Rainer was the only recorded adult little person and adult giant in history.

Various poems from section one appeared individually in *Thimble Literary Magazine*.

TABLE OF CONTENTS

1st act

2nd act

For Betty Soden (mama) the love of my life, and Paul, my partner in crime.

For Ann Howells, who stuck by me.

These poems are for Reverie, Christopher, and Adam. May we all find happy circuses as we go.

—————-first act—————-

one half of a consummation in mist

*-for my son Adam Rainer the only recorded
adult little person and adult giant in history*

Adam, after the first man, if
you are the mango and I am

the leaf and the tree from which
you grew my son but we were

not mother and child but conjoined
twins - boys together at the hip,

what then? Will you drape my
head in a cotton or silk shroud, spare

pashmina covering
hushes echoed over hush

when you go in to make a kiss?
Hugging her, what now offspring

of thine own embrace? Is every
Mother her son's lonely twin,

broken, rent, divot for divot?
Her dimples can not hold you

like my arm. Tell me of the
gender of saviors.

Fair Day or to the river with my Little Fish

-for my son Adam Rainer the only recorded
adult little person and adult giant in history

We came to the circus grounds
by small train, not a toy in the forest,
but the fog swaddled everything.

Between galena tinctured arms of
trees branching to smaller fingerlings
and capillaries of damp brown hair

on the steam engine swam.
Adam and I immersed in it
on the front most wooden bench

holding hands. I whispered this
is where the royals
of divergent evolution reside.

God has many plans and we
are two of them. Better to see the fault
in others and the beauty in ourselves.

Deformity is where and how
the magic enters in.

Mother to son
after seeing the Wolf-Man
exhibition

-for my son Adam Rainer the only recorded
adult little person and adult giant in history

Your father was rather more hairless,
burning the evidence in tawny ripple,
smooth, hard, striated, ochre earth,

purple river of veins.
And from the chalice of his hands
he would drink of me.

When seeds are left all mothers know
the terror of the sky, foreign objects
falling, shooting stars, asteroids

crashing, harm and harm and
helplessness planted deep. He banged
on the glass and it frightened me.

My fear is my only carriage

-for my son Adam Rainer the only recorded
adult little person and adult giant in history

The word rent and the word bill
are the bookends of my life.
Having been your ground and the earth
is a garden of dust

how will you transplant yourself?
Oasis and root and honor
are words starving for example and room
enough to be of service or change.

When I die and I rise and it rains
you will be weightless and you will be cleansed.
Nothing can be destroyed
but remade made love or revisited

clouds our neighbors and the laughter
of holes in roofs pans catching tears.
Adam, should you go to live in the
carnival? In one tent Alligator Woman

lights a fire with her tail, in another The
Cerulean Magician tucks the crowd back
into an antique silk top hat. A woman
walks by that appears to be a giraffe.

we had
to share our hiccups

-for my son Adam Rainer the only recorded
adult little person and adult giant in history

inherent in slow braveries
most secretly revealed
when i was young
i dreamed of breathing fire

before mobs
of incandescent strangers
witnessing the color orange
burn down

the graduation of the night
as i stood
perfume oiled and glistening
before everything and god

the clandestine matters
of my unformed heart
laid bare
a father's voice repeating

black is distance
only when
you haven't crossed it yet
as from behind

memory
and tent-cloth
the snake-boy's eyes appeared
a savage brilliant color red

beyond combustion
erasing guesswork
of what oxygen
hitting blood reveals

reporting from candle-wax man's
autumn colored stateroom tents no. 2

-for my son Adam Rainer the only recorded
adult little person and adult giant in history

the rococo draperies lifted
as a ghost on a moor rings a bell

his skin is a maw
reflexively i squeeze adam's tiny hand

the shirt he removed is a calico
cotton heap on the floor

as if clothing can hold
an opinion about exhaustion

i want to say something good here
about the brown of his eyes

but his skin is the foil
normally left behind

his skin is a maw reflexively i squeeze
adam's nanoscopic hand

my head is a loop
and i may be repeating things

the shirt he removed is a collapsing
hole

he is wrapping material
usually left behind or on the outside

of unopened gifts
truly any god here is one too many

the salt on my lips dries
faster than i can lick

broken shell dry meat-picked
and sapless my throat burns

from an empty theater box my voice
and the sun goes down

adam son of my flesh
less than four feet tall forever

let's watch the candle-man melt
and the sun come up again

next week adam will be eight feet tall
i do not know this then

or the true cost of tickets rides
and viaducts

the fingernails of lesser
deities left digging in your skin

sleep-over one

-for my son Adam Rainer the only recorded
adult little person and adult giant in history

when on the threshold of ourselves
gravity is falling close enough to stance
even planets oval back

dandelions finish playing light-thief
nothing approaches nothingness again
and adam dreams rolled snuggly

in a pendleton by the embers as
the two-headed women shakes her left
in the flame-wash and i think

a symbol for death rises over us
ellipsoid followed by ellipsis haloing
the crossbar of her golden chariot

flint-spark and glimmer in the air
feelings thin and tightly wound
as an immeasurable thought

one ear to the other
the cosmos is a bedroll
the earth a pillow by the fire

patio furniture
sans patio

-for my son Adam Rainer the only recorded
adult little person and adult giant in history

on a table
beside her yurt rests

a plastic version of a finer tea set
between
an evening's pink and purple sky

her pinky pointing out
a clearing runway

the horizon where we scale to something
that has no beginning and no end
finer than escape

sipping oolong tea and listening to edith
piaf with lisbet jonquil the smallest women

who ever lived

the grass is damp with spell
and the oak is in the stars

-for my son Adam Rainer the only recorded
adult little person and adult giant in history

The next tent was ten shades
of blackstrap dim. Entering required
an extra ticket and a sort of genuflection.

Stuffed as a smorgasbord belly
the bethel swelled. Candelabras and brocade
ropes swung in the held breath

and in the candle-wash. They believed
their eyes were on another form of god.
I saw a guardian angel carved as a statue's

face on the back of his marvelous head.
At now over seven-feet tall my son Adam
waited outside still as an oak in a wind.

Inside the man introduced himself by
the legendary name Edward Mordrake
for purposes of anonymity I believe.

Recognizing the crowd mesmerized
and himself the star of this day's panoply
of human marvels slowly he turned

his back on us and I swear even now
the second face said, "not a devil down
but the dew is on the moor".

A Parliament of Owls
(my child at the people show)

-for my son Adam Rainer the only recorded
adult little person and adult giant in history

We came to the Skinny Man
and you wept. How will he cast

a shadow wide enough to hold
a picnic basket sandwich or the

sound of a mouth-harp note held
in wax-paper or a dove in the air?

I had the heart to answer but no
scissors and no knife to cut the

string. Some balloons are long and
thin, no profile but a nose.

Home now and
Imaging myself
Phoolan Devi the Bandit
Queen from Uttar Pradesh brave

-for my son Adam Rainer the only recorded
adult little person and adult giant in history

Or anyone except Adam's mother
Adam dying stretched on the universe
Like a rack
Great wing growing growing
As I spin penniless
Dishrags of imaginary silk overhead
Imagination is where comfort sneaks
Spinning my way to exhaustion
Toes squeaking on linoleum
Lump of sticky dough
For a pillow
Absurd
I lay down in the kitchen

Afraid the oven will burn us all down in the
Night

Adam's Song

-for my son Adam Rainer the only recorded
adult little person and adult giant in history

Now that you are tall, beyond tall,
and nearer to god and death

we have come to the carnival
again. Where will you fit on this

blue stone at seven feet eight
inches tall, three breaths left

and no time for the rhetorical? In
your eye there is a skyscraper,

a sparrow, and a new cloud, the
firmament hardly reaching your crown.

sleep
is an animal that waits

-for my son Adam Rainer the only recorded
adult little person and adult giant in history

i want to write to you about a poet
who came to our latest show

paring and repairing

all the world
into a turn of phrase

words woven to make
the passersby go wild

wading
through the drunk-boys
and the waves

of conscious inner turmoil
hierarchies
of engagement

entertainment
confession
discernment of design
and finally

emotional translation
knowing truly
all poetry is transfiguration

crowd noise
and clabber mouths
bent back

ambient soul
standing on a street corner stealing
spotlights with a laugh

dragging truth and smoke behind
fitzcarraldo's steam boat
over land

mud deep in the jungle's center

stepping up to form a dais
out of open air
sidewalk stippled star-killer
microphone wide as a city
hidden stage revealer

she
(the city)
fingertips smoothing her latest
papier-mâché dress
stopping
when she saw
between the lost people

and the crying knife
the corner where we made our stand

yowling
maps have legends

stopping when she heard

entranced and mumbling
i've seen things you people wouldn't believe

cold enough to see our breath
we made language in the tall grass

on the days the words won't come
we hold hands

—————-second act—————-

Charlie

I am fortunate considering
I cannot actually see the burden
that bought me a lifetime pass
to the grotesque carnival of lost
souls. My uncle Stanley tutored
me in Italian and New Testament
Greek. Together we swam the gorgeous
texts of Measure for Measure,
Frankenstein, Little Women, Ulysses,
Tropic of Capricorn, Moby Dick,
Delta of Venus. I am displayed
in a breech-cloth and necklace
made of teeth. I refuse to growl
and howl, ignoring the extra coin,
choosing instead defiant
silence. They have never heard
of hyperkyphosis or myeloma,
seeing only this camel's hump,
this iceberg rising from my shoulders.
My spine gnarled like taffy,
like ginger root, like a cock's
neck you wring to stop it from
crowing. I have broken each mirror,
I should have simply ignored.
Let them recover their breath,
let them shriek like a Catholic
schoolgirl when she discovers boys

prime the pump. In another life I
was an emperor, they are dolts,
not worthy to shine
my shoes.

Precious

Plenty of the fans remember
"Lullaby League," even if they don't
know how our lives were changed.
No one ever hired so many of us,
certainly not for a mainstream movie.
So we were fictional characters,
with stupid names. So they gave us

ridiculous, cartoony voices. It was
more money then I'd seen in my life.
Solid, respectable work, no more
foolish than the stuff they do today,
for a paycheck. More dignified
than Bridesmaids or Dumb and Dumber.

No one filmed us on the pot. And if we
got carried away after sundown, we never
missed morning call, cocktail flu or not.
Now my family consists of the diminished
and discarded. Grease paint warriors,
rope walkers, sword swallowers, geeks,

the exquisitely broken and extraterrestial
interlopers. Understand, I love my nieces,
my children and their children. But those
who wander alongside bind me with balance
and warmth. I won't lie. When the mob
swarms, I fight not to think. Have I really sunk
to this? After O'Selznick? After Baum? After
prancing with Garland? But the Grannies.

The Aunts who bring their darlings to gape
with awe and curiosity. "Why are you small?
Are you magic?" Yeah. Yeah. Yeah. I know.
It's more disgusting than quaffing honey
straight from the jar. But think about it.

In this rushing, rushing, parade of frantic
humanity to its final, glorious downpour
of chain lightning and frogs
and rain blacker than pitch, I bear
enchantment. Grace like tattered
snowflakes in merciless drought.

hecuba

astonishing to think how easily
i earn my keep lifting my skirt
to reveal curious mingling
of pendulum and pistil
they gussy me up like some
intoxicated poobah on fat pillows
extravagant threads with a hookah
or that caterpillar who toyed
with alice amazed they will pay
me to fuck with their cracker
brains nobody really gets
the mystery of what makes
a lady or bloke and frankly
i learned very early boystuff
held no attraction (though a jock
is handy) the constant need
to defend the swagger
of your balls the grunting
and swearing and tossing
like ignorant apes even i
can thrive as an exotic
dancer if i pile on enough
rouge and green eyeshadow
and flounce like the girlies
but in the end it was too much
work carrying on like little egypt
i dont care if they think i dropped
here from saturn or that im

some kind of reptilian anomaly
when i get home i draw a long scalding
delicious soak in my tub with petals
and eucalyptus i powder and slip
into siamese pajamas i tap
the needle and cook the remarkable
syrup ipushoffipushoff
I push off.

Lobster Boy

My Jewish buddy Sam used to joke
I could wreck a Hassidic wedding
just by showing up and let me
tell you, nothing like a friend
to keep you chuckling through
the rough times. I guess it's no
blinding revelation that the key
to surviving this dark, dark ride
is salvaging your power to detach,
to laugh when they gasp at your
pincers, or when you light a smoke,
or remove your shirt. Maybe tonight
I will find a dance hall, bathed in cool
forgiving darkness except for Christmas
lights twinkling like cheap grace, where
Moonlight Serenade floats the air,
where a sweet, tender girl might grant
me a turn without noticing or caring
I am a crustacean in disguise. Night after
night I read Richard III, envy him
his cynicism, his audacity, his contempt
for idiots who see only his gnarled spine,
his benign demeanor. Imagine the sack
it must have taken to seduce the widow
of the man you murdered. One day
I will say goodbye to my terror,
my cowardice. I will silently glide
among them, sliding my hungry knife
between their ribs like you would
prepare a fat hen for supper.

Alligator Woman

I have never sought water,
outside my tub. There is nothing
miraculous in that splash
and awful sensation of getting
drenched, when caught in a downpour.
My name is Amanda. I suppose
the man who paints my lurid portrait
on that enormous banner must choose
an angle, a depiction that captures
my essence, yet entices the strange
appetite. My teeth are normal. My skin
supple and responsive. When I arrived
with flippers and webbing, my parents
were inappropriately calm. Resigned.
They showed neither pity nor indifference,
helping me sort the everyday
tasks of washing, dressing, heating
a can of soup. I may lack the ethereal
appeal of a mermaid or the breathless
exhilaration of a dolphin. My skills are more
reasonable and practical. I will not pander
to vapid curiosity, but tell you this.
I do not require special appliances
to drive, or smoke. The real money
comes from the sick fucks who bribe me
to their bedrooms. You cannot imagine
the growls. The sobbing. If you want to
know more, buy a ticket. C'mon.
Quench your eyes on the abomination,
the merciful, blue Princess
of the Moon.

Wilbur and Stanley

They ask if our cocks are identical
or if there's something creepy
going on between us, when we
treat them them to dinner, when
we're stupid enough to believe
Plum Wine and Pad Thai might
be the path to genuine friendship.

They insult us without meaning to,
without guessing how ridiculous
they are. Yes, of course, I know
Stanley's shoulder blades, better
than my own. But how many
brothers happily scrub the other's

back? Our pulses sing the splendor
of rhythm in counterpoint, our
sleeping breath a nocturne
of inspiration and exhalation,
drenching our cells with gobs
of oxygen. We dine and sometimes

feed each other. We whisper
and giggle together when sitting
through Ibsen or Strindberg. We piss
our frothy streams in meadows.
We row to the center of an extravagant
blue lake, crooning Flower Duet
or The Pearl Fishers. We drown

in the barker's schtick, as he beckons
the mob: God or Nature saw fit
to join Stanley and Wilbur through
this Valley of Grief, and perhaps
into eternity. I will hold my companion
when another siren breaks his feverish

heart. I will bandage his spindly knee
and massage the dread from his spine.
Stanny, I am your fierce tiger, your man
in the moon. I know they are poised
to devour. They will never know
the most trivial detail about us. Let them
subsist on wet garbage. Let them starve.

Agnes

My sisters navigated this planet
before the first Christian
was sacrificed, carefully arranging
stones for altars, pouring tallow
for illumination, gathering Sweet
Flag and Oleander by moonlight
to coax orbits, elements, pulses,
forging the poetry of spells,
summoning gods of gust
and thunder and placenta
and mountain and those
consorting with shadows.
Some of us became midwives,
some teachers, some managed
on their own, growing herbs
without names, baking small
cakes that could reverse tides
or marriages. I did well in my
town when they learned I was
discreet and could find me
in deepest night to divulge what
waited in the years to come,
or departed kin needed them
to know. When the carnival
wheeled into the square, stirring
my grumbling, brittle bones,
I knew they would jump
at the chance never suspecting

what I actually am. Every reckoning,
every verdict hovering
beside a boy or his uncle,
a wife or her cousin, was louder
than radio, brighter than Indian spice.
Now I enjoy a sacred place
in the wagon. The world has broken
open for me, like a cob doll crafted
for spite. I lay out my future
cards, read the code of hands,
to the comfort of some. I bunk
with the disfigured and malformed,
cosmic sovereigns and the phenomenal
passing for strange and sleep more
soundly than ever I have.

lucille

mamas cycle had hit hard
that sunday morning so lavinia
took me to her church
over the bridge and past
the woods where folks
dug deep for rich notes
of misery and raw unashamed
prayer there was a sharp tingle
in my palms below my ribs
a surge of misery in my feet
when the drops started
i swooned and when i came
to a smiling lady in deep blue
was standing at the altar
holding me in her arms
i guess i was seven
and the congregation carrying
on something fierce
blood staining my easter
dress shine seizing me
like a soaring fever
sometimes it helped to think
the tents were for the circus
as we toured the bible belt
i was twenty six before the crowds
got smaller and smaller
and by then married to nelson
but the miraculous flow just went

on and on i dont blame him
really for leaving i understand
why the bally doesnt use me
to draw the mob or they see
me last some folks cry some
shriek and damned if this
haggard teenaged boy didnt climb
up on the stage and tap my hem
and later they told me the leukemia
was gone

Cornelius

The railroads were built on my
grandfather's back, and the backs
of countless other Chinese
laborers. For crackers too proud
to lift a pickaxe or sledge hammer.
Do they think I cannot hear their
mocking? They know nothing
of my past, or bother to listen.
They cannot comprehend. Instead
they see: The Yellow Kid, Fu Manchu,
Charlie Chan, The Obsequious
Mongoloid Wizard. When I asked
to see the carnival boss, I wore purple
robes. I anointed my throat with oils,
pungent and alluring. "Mr. Jack Maple,
I will conjure the miraculous, and exotic.
Pluck orchids from the invisible
realm, resurrect gentle, cunning
creatures of feather and cold circulation.
No dandy hats or rabbits. No milk
or gamblers cards. For that moment,
intuition eclipsed Jack Maple's reason.
Now I endure ignorance, mixed
with swoons, and sudden inhalation,
and the rough adoration of applause.
It has taken awhile, but I can sniff
out a klansman without effort. They
stomp like thick, enormous beasts,

but once their wives, their frail progeny
soar with fever. Once the clouds drown
this hopeless, spinning leviathan.
They will know, they will know I am
no imposter.

Wilhelmina

The other attractions tell me the mob
pays to see my miniscule noggin maybe twice
the size of an acorn squash ears nearly
wings troglodyte lids my nose
and lips content as any lama
pilgrim. Though I am a lady, despite
my weightless effulgent violet
pinafore and whimsical bow, I lack
the delicate features of womanhood.
My Aunt Jezebel fount me dainty
satin slippers when I serenade
the audience. I know Daisy, Daisy,
and Pirate Jenny and even I Wish
I Could Shimmy. I love how
they laugh and make goony faces.
They can get rowdy but lucky
for me brawls don't cook up
like sometimes with those exotic
ladies from across the wide ocean.
They share their hookah (just us
girls) and play music from the tents
of sultan princes. Genevieve is from Harlem.
I love how the brown paste takes me
sailing. I can strike the terror of a pirate
or prance on a half-moon or swim
with the octopus and electric blue
jellyfish. Aunt Jezebel protects me,
pitches in to pull her weight. Carnival

folk crowd around whenever she stews
up a pot (she gets strange tips from Agnes)
of Rabbit Hash or Black Bone Chili.
Nathan keeps proposing, he calls me
sweet darlin, but auntie looks straight
into my brimming eyes and says please
know I love you, Mina,
and know how it is.

Nathan

ive worked   dairy farms   and cock fights
emergency rooms   and political lobbies
   it sickens   me when i hear   of experimentation
on our animal companions   to make shampoo
   or lipstick   or medicine   why not use prisoners
or those willing   to tolerate   side effects
   for remuneration   i understand   the actual
problem isnt   progress or healing
  its the hubris   of trivializing   creatures
with just   as much purpose   and less   presumption
i wouldnt care   if you caught me   caressing
   their giddy   phenomenal   plumage
or soothing   their frantic   cosmos heads
   dipping and bobbing galactic metronome   i ask you
are there any animals more at ease with the grotesque
  than the sons   of troglodytes   and homoerectus
with their secret clubs to witness creepy   spectacles
ridiculous masks and whips   and ping-pong balls
  they defile themselves and other more noble creatures
while they scorn   my act im sure   this will astonish
you but i love   the chickens i name   and must
   sacrifice   to squeak by   on meager wage
     i know just how   to soothe them
into my mouth   cooing and chanting   i say a prayer
for each one   sally   gladys   gracie   beth
before i crunch   teeth efficient and merciful
     as the guillotine

Josh

I am made of chalk, ephemeral
as moonbeam, my scalp
a sprouted nimbus of delicate
dandelion follicles. First you
discover the scalding kiss
of sunshine, the intense gaze
and unabashed gawking
of strangers, eruption
of confused, spontaneous
laughter. The children tugging
their parents sleeves, hushing
and slow wagging of heads.
My eyes, dazzling irises
have come from Saturn,
translucent layers ringing
a fierce red cauldron
of marvels. Next you learn
the rush of haunting the familiar
places where the dull-witted
gather, sporting cool, unexpected
colors like magenta and lavender,
the dark aviators and panama hat.
Third, you dip long and thirstily
in the exhilarating spring of self-
adoration. Gulping. Quenching.
Slaking. In this you are no different
from everyday mammals. Flaunt

your extraordinary birth. Then
when barker cues you to strip
entirely, bask in the revelation
of your spectral glory.

Sebastian

My mother called me her scrawny,
stewing chicken with ironic,
but earnest affection. She was genius
with a Bernina, sneaking out
my suits and trousers and tunics
when she left her shift
in the garment district. Managing
on a breakfast of strong coffee
and Lucky Strikes. She dragged
me out of bed for temple, baked
special sweets for my bar mitzvah,
and treated me whenever the modest,
tawdry circus pitched outside the city
limits. Maybe a year after I became
a teenager my sparse body took
a ghoulish turn, though miraculously
she never seemed to notice. Her
delectable cooking increased
exponentially and though I gobbled
with ferocity, my skin held tighter,
like the soul reluctant to leave
our chaotic mix of bliss
and apoplexy. After mama passed
I continued to visit the circus where
this congenial guy said he'd ply me
with rich sausage and knish.
He offered a job, slowly gathering
I didn't understand. Tact was not

his inclination. You could pass
for The Grim Reaper, he said.
He wasn't exactly thrilled, comforting
another man in public, but I was
bawling so loudly I guess
he didn't mind. When he introduced me
to the other sons and daughters
of radiant misfortune, who grinned
and chuckled, never grimacing or looking
away, I returned with my suitcase.

Victor

I hitched a ride with another
guy my age, Trevor. The longer
we drove, the closer we got, sharing
disappointments and shame, deep
into the night hours, listening
to wailing, disconsolate crooners
on channels like Cowboy Life
and Coyote Howl and Broken Spur.
We'd eat in empty diners, follow
each other to the gent's toilet.
Sometimes urgency eclipses
proclivity. Trevor ignored another
stop light, and didn't last long
after colliding with a blue Mustang.
The driver stomped over to kick
his ass, but the twisted, careening
mashup that shattered my jaw,
scattered my molars and tilted
my eyes, were too much for the guy.
I will spare you the obvious
comparisons to Picasso, DeKooning
and Bacon. The next driver who pulled
over, led a carnival caravan filled
with convivial outsiders, destined
for glamour and grief. My decision
was clear. Where else could I go?
Sometimes I sneak off with Gregory
and Philip, and we delight

in our naked boy time. Groaning
and purring. I'm not going to
bore you with stories of my past
predatory habits, though I've
come to reconsider the scratching
and shrieking and hot spittle
burning my cheek. The women I
degraded with poisonous spunk.
I cannot be with girls
anymore. Not ever.

Barney

I could never resist
the violent cracking. The planet
drum of sudden downpour.
They bill me as Lightning Rod.
Seven times. *Seven times:*
I've been chosen. Atomic
particles of marrow sizzling
like water drops
on a cast iron skillet. My brain
poaching like an egg.
The barker introduces me
with incomparable shtick.
Then the sneers. The chatter
and chuckles. Then the rough stuff.
I shut my eyes. I raise
my hands, like Pontius Pilate
pronouncing a verdict,
after ablution. I sing
in Aramaic. The birds
observe a silence.
Humming, blue radio
waves, strike the anvil,
hidden deep within their ears.
Their hair floats. Joints turn
to ice. Muscles convulse. Nails
go black. I will annihilate
them, one by one. I will
swim the perpetual
ocean of night.

Drusilla

It's the guys that offer to buy you
supper, when they can already
see you're eating. He almost
seems surprised I use a fork
and spoon. That I take my time.

Then it's clear he's watching
carefully, carefully as I chew
every bite. Hoping I'll change
expression, or make some
disgusting noise. He reaches for

a handkerchief to dab glistening
streaks of sweat, to blot
his trembling lips. So. Yeah.
I accept his invitation
to a tony hotel. Where he

will call room service, to lay
out a table with two
chairs, and Limoges,
and Baccarat, and blue linen
so pale you might believe
it was cut from the sky.

It might be easier if my host
weren't persistently tucking
his hands in his lap. As if

I didn't know precisely what
he's touching. As if I were
incapable of intelligent exchange

of ideas. If I mention Man Ray
or Duchamp or Kahlo, I cannot tell
if he's startled, or merely bewildered.
I am far too ungainly to find
this distracting or quaint,
and I've had enough. Whatever

his education, he's still a cornpone.
Pathetically lost by the revelations
you find at a planetarium. Incapable
of grasping enigmas surpassing
the perimeters of his wee brain.

Like the Magi I come bearing
gifts. Simple yet remarkable.
Clothes pins, nylon rope, chloroform,
blindfold, gag. I do not want to hear
a whimper, a sob, a howl, a plea.

My mother taught me the craft
of sailor's knots, and conquest.
Testing the limits of excruciation.
She taught me how to tilt
the cosmos like a steaming cup
of Chai to my lips.

Paul Koniecki lives and writes in Dallas, Texas. He was once chosen for the John Ashbery Home School Residency. His poems feature in Richard Bailey's movie "One of the Rough" distributed by AVIFF Cannes. His previous books are available from Kleft Jaw Press, NightBallet Press, Dark Particle Press, Spartan Press, and Between Shadows Press. Paul proudly sits on the editorial board of *Thimble Literary Magazine*. His poems have appeared in *ENTROPY, Gasconade Review, As It Ought To Be Magazine, River Dog, Blue Max Review, Chantarelle's Notebook,* and many more.

Christopher Stephen Soden received his MFA in Poetry from Vermont College of Fine Arts in January of 2005. He teaches craft, theory, genre and literature. He writes poetry, plays, literary, film and theatre critique for sharpcritic.com and EdgeDallas. Christopher's poetry collection, Closer was released by Rebel Satori Press on June 14th, 2011. He received a Full Fellowship to Lambda Literary's Retreat for Emerging LGBT Voices in August 2010. His performance piece: Queer Anarchy received The Dallas Voice's Award for Best Stage Performance. Water and A Christmas Wish were staged at Bishop Arts and Every Day is Christmas. In Heaven at Nouveau 47. Other honors include: Distinguished Poets of Dallas, Poetry Society of

America's Poetry in Motion Series, Founding Member, President and President Emeritus of The Dallas Poets Community. His work has appeared in: *Rattle, The Cortland Review, 1111, Typishly, F(r)iction, G & L Review, Chelsea Station, Glitterwolf, Collective Brightness, A Face to Meet the Faces, Resilience, Ganymede Poets: One, Gay City 2, The Café Review, The Texas Observer, Sentence, Borderlands, Off the Rocks, The James White Review, The New Writer, Velvet Mafia, Poetry Super Highway, Gertrude, Touch of Eros, Gents, Bad Boys and Barbarians, Windy City Times, ArLiJo, Best Texas Writing*